Crane and Pelican

A Bird Book for Kids™

By Novare Lawrence

Nada Bindu Publishing Co.

The contents of this book previously appeared in the digital-only editions *Crane: A Bird Book for Kids* and *Pelican: A Bird Book for Kids*.

First Print Edition – June 2017

ISBN-10: 1-63307-014-X
ISBN-13: 978-1-63307-014-1

Published by:
Nada Bindu Publishing Co.
Carson City, NV 89703
Website: www.nadabindupublishing.com
Email: inquiries@nadabindupublishing.com

To My Readers

Crane and Pelican _is my fourth paperback book, a format which highlights the truly beautiful pictures of these birds and their lives. These two birds first appeared as their own e-books which have been combined without change here into this printed volume. The number of e-books in the_ **_A Bird Book for Kids_** _series now numbers eleven and counting._

I invite your comments and reviews on the website where you bought this book. This will help me to continue to create books of the highest quality and enjoyment for all my readers. Along with your review, please let me know what other birds you would like to see as I continue to expand this series, as e-books first and as paperback editions that combine two e-books into a single printed book.

Many Thanks,
Novare Lawrence

CONTENTS

Crane

Cranes are tall and elegant looking birds with thin, bare legs, a streamlined body and a long thin neck. Cranes are the tallest birds that fly, and some cranes are among the heaviest too.

A sandhill crane taking off

The heaviest cranes are the Siberian and red-crowned cranes, both weighing in at about 35 lb (15 kg). The heaviest flying bird in the world is the kori bustard, found in Africa, which may reach a weight of 45 lb (21 kg). The kori bustard and these two largest species of cranes all have wingspans reaching up to 10 feet (3 m). The kori bustard, however, does not fly very far at all, preferring to run on the ground while most crane species are migratory, flying long distances with the change of seasons.

Siberian cranes and a red-crowned crane

There are fifteen species of cranes. Although other birds, like herons, ibis, and flamingos look similar in appearance, cranes are different from those other birds. If you see a large bird flying with a long, straight neck and straight legs, it is probably a crane. Flamingos fly with a straight neck but have pink legs and a short, curved beak. Herons, egrets and even pelicans fly with their long necks curved into an S-shape.

A heron, flamingo and egret flying

The many species of cranes are spread out across every country around the world except in South America and Antarctica. Cranes require a body of water and large open areas in which to live, find food and reproduce. Most cranes roost in wetlands where water is shallow and they can build nests on grassy mounds or dry shores. Two species of cranes, the African black-crowned and grey-crowned cranes, roost in trees.

A mated pair of sandhill cranes and their nest with two eggs

Compared to most other birds, cranes have a long lifespan. The red-crowned crane may live forty years in the wild, while in captivity they have been known to live for seventy years. Also long-lived is the albatross, a large sea bird which can spend years away from land. They may live up to sixty years in the wild. The oldest bird living in captivity was a cockatoo that lived to be 80 years old.

A red-crowned or Japanese crane

Male and female cranes tend to look the same, unlike many other bird species such as peacocks and ostriches where males and females vary in both size and color. Male adult cranes may be slightly bigger than females but it is not easy to tell them apart.

Male and female black-crowned cranes look identical

Among the fifteen different species, cranes vary greatly in size. The small demoiselle crane found in Central Eurasia is only 3 feet (91 cm) tall while the sarus crane found in India and Southeast Asia can be almost 6 feet (1.8 m) tall. The lighter demoiselle crane, only 6 pounds (2.7 kg) in weight, migrates from China and Mongolia down to India and Africa. The much bigger sarus crane, weighing 3 to 4 times more than the demoiselle crane, does not migrate long distances.

The small demoiselle crane

The fifteen different types of cranes are divided into four groups. In one group, called the crowned cranes, are black-crowned and grey-crowned cranes; both have stiff golden feathers on their heads. Cranes in the other three groups are known as typical cranes. One group is very large and contains the common or Eurasian crane, sandhill, whooping, sarus, brolga, Siberian, white-naped, hooded, black-necked, and red-crowned cranes. The remaining two groups are small with the blue and demoiselle crane in one, and the wattled crane in a group by itself.

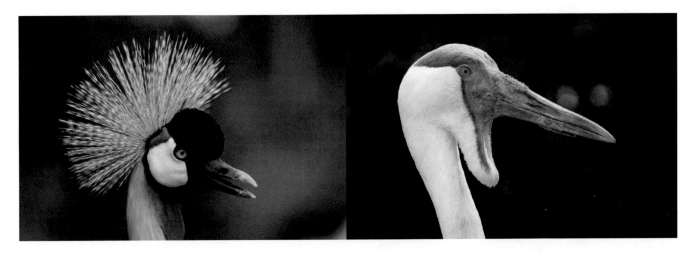

A grey-crowned crane's golden head feathers and a wattled crane named for its extended throat wattle

Cranes communicate with each other through a variety of methods. One method is the different calls or sounds that they make. Sandhill cranes, found in North America and Siberia, are particularly famous for their loud trumpeting call which can be heard over a long distance. Trumpeting is part of the courtship and bonding ritual as the male and female call back and forth to each other.

Male and female sandhill cranes dancing and calling to each other

Another way cranes communicate is through their skin color. Most cranes have patches of bare skin on their faces. Those patches of skin can be expanded and contracted and may become more brightly colored to express emotions to other cranes.

A black-crowned crane showing a pink patch of skin on its face

The demoiselle and blue cranes, which do not have bare skin patches, communicate another way. They can raise the feathers on their heads up and down. Wattled cranes and other bird species like cockatoos have this same ability as well.

A demoiselle crane up close

Cranes are noted around the world for their courtship rituals which are a very important communication method for male and female bonding. Cranes typically mate for life. During mating season especially, they renew their relationship through dances and calls. The red-crowned crane has a particularly elegant dance, also called a duet. The male and female circle around each other, jumping up and down while spreading their wings until they come close to each other. At this point they both throw their heads back and trumpet together.

A mated pair of red-crowned cranes performing a duet

Cranes mature between the ages of two and three and soon begin looking for a mate. Some cranes, however, may not form a lifetime bond until as late as seven years of age. Depending on the species, cranes may stay in large groups or they may break off into small colonies when they prepare their nests. Each species of crane has its own preferences in nesting, food and bonding rituals.

A sandhill crane family

Sandhill cranes, which are found in North America, perform a duet where the male calls once and the female calls back two times. They perform this bonding year round, not just during mating season. During the winter, sandhill cranes may congregate with other cranes in groups of 10,000 or more.

A mated pair of sandhill cranes looking for food together

The male and female sandhill cranes construct their nest together. They build it in marshes or bogs by creating a dry mound for the eggs. The female lays one to three eggs. The eggs are dull brown in color with red markings. They hatch after about thirty days. Like quail or geese, crane chicks hatch with eyes open and are covered in downy feathers. This means that they can leave the nest after less than a day. The chicks are fed often by both parents during the first three weeks. Parents feed their chicks until they are around nine to ten months old by which time the chicks are mostly independent.

A sandhill crane on the nest with two chicks

Sandhill cranes feed by pushing their bills into the ground or shallow water looking for seeds and other foods. While they eat mostly plants, sandhill cranes can eat a variety of things like berries, insects, snails, reptiles, frogs and other amphibians. To prepare for migrations, they may also eat plants grown by farmers, such as corn and wheat, to get more calories which are needed for long days of flying. Sandhill cranes often migrate in groups of a hundred or more.

A small group of sandhill cranes flying together

The whooping crane is the only other crane species living in North America. This crane species became severely endangered due to hunting and the loss of its habitat. Less than 25 whooping cranes were alive in 1941 and this inspired people to begin conservation efforts to prevent the extinction of the species. In 2011, their numbers had increased to almost 600, with about one-third of those living in captivity. Conservation efforts continue today but it is still considered to be endangered.

A whooping crane with a favorite food - crab

Whooping cranes can live up to 24 years in the wild. They are tall, reaching 5 feet (1.5 m) with a wingspan of 7.5 feet (2.3 m). Mated pairs perform a very rhythmic duet in the mornings, calling back and forth to each other. The female lays one or two eggs during breeding season on a dry mound in marshy territory. The eggs weigh about 6.7 oz. (190 grams) which makes them about 7 times lighter than an ostrich egg but about 4 times heavier than an average chicken egg. Whooping crane eggs are olive-colored. The parents, usually the mother, feed the chicks for up to 8 months. The chicks are completely independent by the time they are one year old.

A young cinnamon-colored whooping crane with identification bands

Whooping cranes are omnivorous meaning that they regularly eat most types of foods. In their Texas wintering grounds, this species feeds on shrimp, mollusks, fish, eel, berries, small reptiles and aquatic plants. Common foods eaten during summer breeding season include frogs, small rodents, fish, aquatic insects, crayfish, clams, snails, aquatic tubers, and berries.

A whooping crane loses its meal

The small demoiselle cranes also perform a bonding display dance and call and response with their partner. They stand up straight, throw their heads back and point their beaks skyward as they call to each other. Demoiselle cranes live in dry grasslands in Mongolia and Northern China but usually stay close to any available streams, rivers, shallow lakes, or other types of wetlands. They eat plants, insects, peanuts, beans, cereal grains, and even small animals.

A very pretty demoiselle crane

In nesting areas, demoiselle cranes prefer patchy vegetation where they can lay their eggs and still be able to see around their nest easily. Females usually lay two eggs which hatch 27-29 days later. Both male and female cranes sit on the eggs but the male takes the primary role to defend the nest from any possible predator. Chicks fledge (first flight) at only 55-65 days, which is the shortest time for any crane species. Demoiselle cranes are the second most abundant crane species.

There's no special nest for the demoiselle crane

The Eurasian crane is also called the common crane because it is the most common crane species. They nest primarily in bogs, swampy meadows, and other shallow freshwater lands found near forests. They like to live in large isolated wetlands, away from people, but will settle for smaller wetlands near farm lands if necessary. During the winter, they look for tall grassland where they will molt which means that they lose old flight feathers and grow new ones. At these times, they will usually group together in large numbers.

Eurasian cranes flocking together in winter to molt

The Eurasian crane builds a nest out of piles of wetland vegetation that the male and female gather. Females usually lay 2 eggs which hatch after 28-31 days. Eurasian crane chicks fledge at 65-70 days. Eurasian cranes eat insects, wild and farmed grain, acorns, frogs, lizards, snakes and rodents. During the winter months, they eat mostly plants.

A Eurasian or common crane hunting

Red-crowned cranes find mates and nest in large wetland areas of Northeast Asia but spend their winters near rivers and freshwater marshes in Japan, China, and Korea. They like to feed in deeper water than other cranes but may look for food in coastal salt marshes, rivers, freshwater marshes, rice paddies, and even cultivated fields. Red-crowned cranes generally don't mind colder temperatures. Those in Japan tend to stay year round while others migrate from Korea or eastern China to as far as Eastern Siberia. Red-crowned cranes are endangered with less than three thousand estimated to be living in the wild.

Red-crowned cranes don't mind feeding in deeper water than other cranes

Red-crowned cranes are well known for their beautiful dancing and bonding display. Starting the dance, the male jumps and calls. The female then joins in, calling back twice for each single male call. During the breeding season, both help to build a dry nest on wet ground or in very shallow water. Females lay two eggs which hatch 29-34 days later. The chicks fledge at around 95 days old. Red-crowned cranes eat a wide variety of insects, fish, amphibians, and rodents, as well as reeds, grasses, berries, corn and grain.

Red-crowned cranes dancing with each other

Black-crowned cranes live across a large region of Africa which includes the upper Nile River in the north and the Atlantic coast of Senegal to the west. Black-crowned cranes live in both wet and dry areas but they prefer freshwater marshes and grasslands, or the edges of lakes and rivers. Black-crowned cranes have two types of calls. The main one is a booming call where the crane inflates the throat sac underneath its chin and pushes the air out while tilting its head backward. The crane also creates a strong honking sound that is very different from the loud, bugle-type calls of other crane species.

A black-crowned crane standing in front of a grey-crowned crane

Black-crowned cranes build circular nest mounds made from grasses and reeds in and around wetlands where they can be hidden from view. Females lay two to five eggs and both male and female sit on the eggs for about 28-31 days. Black-crowned crane chicks fledge at 60-100 days, which is the longest time of any of the cranes. Both parents guard the nest, at times watching from a nearby tree in order to better see the surrounding area. Black-crowned and grey-crowned cranes are the only cranes able to roost in trees because they have a longer toe on the back of their feet that helps them to grab onto tree branches.

A pair of black-crowned cranes eating together

Cranes naturally keep their distance from people as they tend to like lots of space and shallow swampy areas to live and feed. Unfortunately, even these places are being reduced in size due to the ongoing need for new human housing and farming lands. As a result, many species of cranes are on the threatened or endangered species lists, including the whooping crane, Siberian crane, and grey-crowned and red-crowned cranes. Efforts are being made in many countries to save lands where the cranes migrate to and from, including important breeding and feeding areas.

Cranes need lots of space, like these grey-crowned cranes on the plains in Africa

Cranes are beautiful, tall, and graceful birds that have been appreciated by many cultures throughout history. Cranes display much affection to each other in their bonding dances so people have seen them as an example of devotion to a life partner. Some cultures, such as Native Americans and Koreans, perform traditional crane dances to celebrate love and life. Cranes also show up in artwork as an example of elegance and beauty.

Close-up of beautiful crane feathers, crane artwork from a temple, and a crane sculpture in China

In Japanese paper folding, called Origami, the crane is a symbol of eternal youth and happiness. It is said that if you make a wish and then make a thousand origami cranes, your wish will be granted. We can all wish for cranes to have space for their dances, places for their nests, and water and food to raise their young. By protecting our endangered cranes, we will always be able to hear the cranes calling out to each other and to us.

A red Origami Crane - Meeting a grey-crowned crane

Pelican

Pelicans are large, funny looking seabirds. They have a long beak with a large flexible throat pouch used to scoop up fish. They waddle from side-to-side when they walk and can be quite curious and almost nosey when it comes to dealing with other animals, including humans.

An Australian Pelican and friend

There are eight species of pelicans around the world. They live in coastal areas and around island groups such as the Galapagos in the Pacific Ocean and the Seychelles east of Africa in the Indian Ocean. Pelicans can be found on every continent except Antarctica. They also live in inland waterways away from the ocean.

Australian Pelicans on the beach and Great White Pelicans inland

Pelicans can be grouped into two categories. Four of the pelicans -- the American White, the Great White, the Australian and the Dalmatian -- have mostly white feathers and build their nests on the ground. The other four -- the Brown, the Spot-billed, the Pink-backed and the Peruvian -- have more grey, brown or black feathers and they build their nests in trees.

A Spot-billed Pelican and a group of Pink-backed Pelicans

Pelicans prefer mild to warm climates so some pelicans migrate from north to south with the seasons. The American White Pelican stays in central Canada during the summer and migrates down to Mexico and Central America in the winter. The Brown Pelican moves up and down the east and west coasts of North America as needed to find its primary food source, fish.

Pelicans flying in formation

Most pelican species are large birds with wingspans longer than most people are tall from head to toe. The adult Dalmatian Pelican can weigh 33 pounds (15 kg) with a wingspan reaching almost 10 feet (3 m). The smallest, the Brown Pelican, may only weigh 6 pounds (2.7 kg) and have a wingspan of just 6 feet (1.8 m) from wingtip to wingtip.

A Dalmatian Pelican flying

Pelicans big and small are very comfortable on the water. They have air sacs in their skin and bones which help them to float very well. Because of these air sacs, more of their body stays above the water than most other sea birds. The air sacs on the skin may also help protect them when they dive into the water to catch fish.

A Brown Pelican floating high in the water

Pelicans also have a special oil gland near the base of their tail which they rub with the back of their heads or their beaks. They spread this oil on to their feathers to help keep them waterproof. This is why you see water drops roll easily off of sea birds. If their feathers soaked up too much water, the birds might become too heavy to swim or take off from the water. Pelicans preen their feathers daily.

A Pelican preening its feathers

Pelicans have another feature that helps them while in the water - their large, fully webbed feet. Pelicans do not tend to stay out on the open ocean like some sea birds. They prefer to fish along the coastlines and often float on the water with other pelicans to rest or watch for small fish near the surface.

Big webbed feet

Pelicans hunt in deep and shallow water but use different techniques. In deeper water, they may plunge dive into the water to catch fish swimming down below the water's surface. Brown Pelicans, in particular, are good at this sort of fishing. In shallow water, where the fish are closer to the surface, several pelicans will join together, flying in single file or v-formation. They scoop up water and fish all together as they glide just inches above the water.

Brown Pelicans diving down to catch fish

Pelicans are strong flyers and their wings are perfectly built for gliding and soaring. They like to follow the thermal air currents that build up between land and sea. As they glide from thermal to thermal they reach higher and higher altitudes. They may reach altitudes of up to 10,000 feet (3048 m) before turning to soar out over the water. Pelicans can travel out as many as 90 miles (145 km) or more every day to find fish.

Big wings help the Pelican glide through the air

Pelicans will also fly in V-formations, like geese, so that those not in the lead don't have to flap as hard as the leader. Gliding and using the V-formation allows the pelicans to conserve energy when flying longer distances. The lead pelican trades places with another pelican every so often so that it can use less energy flying in the back with the others.

Pelicans flying together

It's quite a sight to see just how steadily a pelican glides with its large wings. Pelicans often glide together just inches above the water as they search for fish right below the surface. They flap their wings a few times and then glide, never touching the water unless they find a school of fish.

Pelicans gliding just inches above the water

The longest bill of any bird in the world is the 1-1/2 foot long (46 cm) bill of the Australian Pelican. A pelican's bill is yellow in color. During the breeding season, their bill, throat pouch and facial skin may become more brightly colored to help attract a mate. The male and female American White Pelicans grow a semi-circular bump in the middle of their top bill. After the pair mate and the female lays her eggs, the bump goes away.

The Australian Pelican with its long bill

A male and female pelican mate for only one season unlike some other birds, such as parrots, that mate for life. Pelicans often nest in colonies that can be as large as 10,000 birds or more. The four ground nesting species choose sandy or grassy areas near the water to build their nests. There is no courtship ritual for these pelicans. The males typically chase a female until she chooses one of them.

A colony of Pelicans showing brightly colored faces and bills during breeding season

For the tree nesting species, the male usually stands alone in the tree. He tries to attract a female pelican to choose him just based on how good he looks. The trees are usually quite close to the water and usually support more than one nest.

Pelicans nesting in a tree top

Before they mate, the male and female pelican first select a nesting site. They then build the nest together, or in the case of the tree-nesting pelicans, simply repair an existing nest from the prior year. The female lays one to three eggs, which both parents incubate for 30 to 60 days. But it's not easy being a pelican chick. For 95% of nests, only one chick survives to hatch, fledge and mature to adulthood.

A Pelican with baby chicks

Ground nesting pelican chicks will often group together with the other chicks after about 25 days. Each chick continues to be fed by its own parents. The parent regurgitates food into their own throat pouch and allows the chick to feed from it. After 40 to 45 days, the chicks may begin to practice swimming and exploring together. At this stage, chicks may accept food from any adult. After about three months, both ground and tree nesting pelican chicks will fledge and begin to find food for themselves.

Pelican chicks getting food from a parent

After fledging, the young pelicans may stay with their parents for a while to learn the best ways to find and catch fish. They mature at three or four years old and then begin to look for their own mates during breeding season. In the wild, pelicans typically live up to 25 years. Pelicans kept in zoos have been known to live twice as long as that.

Pelican parent and child

Pelicans are good at fishing and are often seen following fishing boats. Fishermen sometimes view them as competition. While an adult pelican may eat four pounds (1.8 kg) of fish a day, that's only a fraction of what fishing boats and large nets can catch.

Peruvian Pelicans watch the fishing boats

Pelicans need fish to survive and this competition over fish is one major issue affecting them. The loss of safe habitats during breeding season, impact of oil spills and increased pollution are other problems that threaten the health and survival of pelicans. Two species, the Spot-billed and Peruvian pelicans, are considered to be Near Threatened status and the Dalmatian pelican is considered as Vulnerable.

Pelicans rest on a fishing boat at anchor

Pelicans like to eat fish but they will eat other things too if necessary. This includes insects, crabs, shrimp, frogs, turtles and even other small birds. Pelicans cannot store food in their throat pouch -- they have to swallow it after catching it before they can fly away.

A Pink-backed Pelican with a fish in its throat pouch

When a pelican scoops a fish out of the water, they first have to force the water back out of their throat pouch without letting the fish get away. It can be tricky and other seabirds like seagulls often steal their catch as their beak opens to let the water out. Larger pelicans can hold up to three gallons (11.4 liters) of water in their pouch. They never fly with food in their pouch; they always swallow it after catching it.

A close-up view of a pelican's throat pouch

Pelicans have a very short tongue so it doesn't get in the way while catching fish. And they can't use their short tongue to move the fish around when it's in their throat pouch. So after the water is gone, sometimes they have to flip the fish into the air and catch it again just right so that they can swallow it easily.

Tossing the fish – the hook on the end of the bill helps to grab the slippery fish

Because pelicans are found all over the world, most cultures have them in their mythology and religious history. In Egypt, Australia and Peru, pelican figures were used on ancient pottery and in paintings. In medieval Europe, the pelican was used as the symbol of a caring parent in family coats-of-arms, badges and pendants. The pelican is also the state bird of Louisiana in the southern U.S. and the national bird of Romania in central Europe and three other countries in the Caribbean.

An Australian Pelican

Pelicans are a unique species with their long bills, elastic throat pouches, air sacs and large wingspans. They may at times look goofy when waddling on the ground with their mouths open and throat pouches flapping. But they can also be graceful and majestic as they dive into the water or glide inches above the surface. Look for them around coastal fishing towns, sharing the fishing grounds with people as they have for thousands of years.

ABOUT THE AUTHOR

Novare Lawrence loves researching and writing books about Nature. She shares the knowledge and beauty of our natural world with kids young and old hoping that we will all do our part to help preserve our planet and all the wonderful species upon it.

You may learn more about her books and the *A Bird Book for Kids*™ series at her website:

ABirdBookforKids.com

And at NadaBinduPublishing.com

A Bird Book for Kids™ Books   by Novare Lawrence

Digital:

Print:

Made in the USA
San Bernardino, CA
12 January 2020